TWO ESSE

Frederic Vanson
Mervyn Linford

To Michael,

from Frederic, by proxy!

With best wishes for your

own literary efforts,

From Olive,

Christmas 1993

BRENTHAM PRESS

First published 1993 by
Brentham Press, 40 Oswald Road, St Albans, Herts AL1 3AQ

ISBN 0 905772 38 5

British Library Cataloguing-in-Publication Data
A catalogue record for this book is available from the British Library

Printed in England by The Ipswich Book Company, The Drift, Nacton Road, Ipswich,
Suffolk IP3 9QR

1 Another City

FREDERIC VANSON

For Christopher Fry
– a wordmaster

Frederic Vanson published more than twenty poetry collections
and contributed to a variety of journals including
Contemporary Review, Country Life, New Poetry,
Outposts, Poetry Review, Tablet etc. His work has
also appeared in anthologies and has been broadcast
on national and local radio. He was for many years
poetry columnist to *Essex Countryside* and edited
In Praise of Essex (Egon Publications).
A former lecturer in English and Liberal Studies, he
retired to Walton on Naze where he died in July 1993 –
sadly, just as this new collection was in preparation.

Another City contains 35 previously unpublished poems, written
as a sequence in traditional sonnet form, together with
a selection of verses *In the Chinese Manner* (Hub, 1972).

CONTENTS

GRANDFATHER

A bull-broad man my grandfather, and one
Who knew a hawk from a heronshaw, could tell
An elm from a wych; a greenhanded man
For whom things prospered in pots or gardens,
Who knew when to plant, prune or pick,
Who gathered chrysanthemums in armfuls
For my grandmother's pleasure, who smoked
A pipe like a bonfire as he watched the sun go down.

Thirty years a townsman, he wrought at the forge
All manner of gadgetry, compelling white iron true
To his hands' will with unconscious artistry;
Yet he had never forgotten the Kentish lore
He grew to, so that bullfinch and wren were familiars,
And known the singular ways that green things grew.

SOUTH WIND

You, South Wind, bless the flower, ripen the velvet peach
Awaken after a cold spring a sudden glory of blossom.
But will you, breathing on me, in Mediterranean kindness
Darken the white hairs at my temples, make smooth my brow?

FAMILY MATTER

Mother, being beautiful, was always right,
Uprightness suffered martyrdom on her brow,
She sniffed contempt for all the baser passions
And with an ice-blue eye kept sex at bay.
The sins of the mother were visited on the children
Who met her terms for what they thought was love.

Impossible for them ever to believe
Any perfection possible than their own.
Was not their lifestyle all a living proof
Of their right thinking as all things fell out
Well for them, children, houses, mortgages, jobs?
The unconforming sister and their father
Were necessary scapegoats. These alone
Saw that the idol stood on feet of stone.

FIRST LOVE

Learning from you what woman-ness is, or may be,
That subtly strange, that then still-undiscovered
Something apart, that magnetism of difference,
Was to find new lands, to be a discoverer
Carried on fair winds to a plenitudinous shore.
So, first of my long-ago loves, I remember
The spun-gold metaphor of your hair, your eyes
Transmoding the old prose world to poetry.

Woman, whose patterns of thought are oblique, uncharted!
Lover and mother to us, demander and giver,
Madonna and temptress, you are all contradictions
And all reconciliations. For the poet in us
Inspirer, for the hunter in us quarry and tamer,
Are Mother of God, are Eve, or Ruth, faithful-hearted.

VOYEURISM

Towards you, and you only, I am voyeurist.
Our years have not lessened my love of seeing you
Reflected in mirrors doubling, trebling your image.
Artist, you have no tabu of the body
When morning light is through the curtains filtering
Shadowing your body's contours as you rise,
I'm freshly familiar with your breasts, your thighs,
Know how you look fastening a bra or stocking.

Familiarity breeds not contempt
But constant wonder and most tender care.
Memory is stored with images I hoard
And can, in an instant, lovingly retrieve –
Yourself be-ringed and dressed, as they say, to kill
Or nude and new and innocent as Eve.

SECRET JOYS

It's fashionable nowadays to sneer
At childhood theophanies and to reduce
Those early years to playground wars and chalking
Crude words on factory walls or to suppose
First love a clumsy groping in the park.
Depicting youth as pimples, lust and farts
May please the cynic, win a quick applause,
But is it true? Well, not for all of us.

True, we did fight, and lusted with our eyes
Miss Prendergast who tried to teach us art,
But there was more, was wonder at the vast
Extent of knowledge. Some hugged secret joy
At how the swan moved on the summer lake
Or watched with tenderness some butterfly.

WORD AND REALITY

The impetuous lover, pacing the forest floor,
Carves his beloved's name on a tree.
His passion dies but the name grows;
Such is the difference between word and reality.

TWO WOMEN

Chasseriau's *Esther* - the eternal siren!
Deliciousness is promised by her plump
And sexy arms, lifted to raise those breasts
Perfect and rose-nippled; her slender waist
Her shadowed navel, her abundance of golden
Uplifted hair, the little mouth that surely
Asks to be kissed and tasted, most of all
The astonishing blue of her wide, lucent eyes.

But Memlinc's *Batsheba* rising from her bed!
A plain and peasant face, her small high breasts
Flat-nippled as a boy, her bulging belly,
Her long shank reaching for an ugly slipper,
Her small, plain hand devoid of jewel or ring,
Could these compel a ruthless, randy king?

HELLENISM

In serried ranks we learned about those Greeks
Who worshipped that sly, partial goddess Athena,
Wore chitons, talked in squares, had slaves to tend them,
Grew olives, drank much wine and knew their Homer.

Later we heard of Plato's fallacy
That but to know the good was surely to love it,
Of Aristotle's mean, of the catharsis,
Of Aeschylus and Aristophanes.

Though far in time from us that sunsoaked city
(Philosophers disputing fancy boys,
Downing the ouzo knowing they would rue it)
Like the old Greeks we too sit on our arses
Talking too much, setting the world to rights,
And, knowing the good, make sure we do not do it.

ONCE IT WAS EASY

Once it was easy with Plato, Darwin, Renan,
With Baudelaire, with *Golden Bough*, with Freud,
A ragbag of private scholarship. Seventeen,
We knew the sickness and the answers too –
More cash, more libraries, more sex, more schools,
And down with banks and dividends and guns;
The world was full of dolts and crooks and fools,
But let us loose and soon the day was won!

Once it was simple until, single spies,
Came doubts, came sorrows, losses, failures, follies,
Experience teaching what no shilling tome
Had ever taught. What then could Plato's ghost
Do, or what Renan's Jesus in his gown?
What scholarship, when Satan rode to town?

TWO ANSWERS

"Tell me," said the child, "tell me the reason why
The bird flies, the sun shines, the grass is green".
Said the philosopher "Child, your question is meaningless".
Said the poet, "Because they love".

SUBURBIA

In those far Betjemanian days Saturdays were
For golfing and plus-fours while laundered and coiffed women
Extended rayon legs from deckchairs on summer lawns,
And hidden by a screen of alders the players
Plop-plopped at tennis until time for tea.
Badged pampered Baby Austins sat by the kerb,
The two-valve portable carried foxtrot and tango
From Brookman's Park or distant Daventry.

The lawns are scrubby now, the stucco peeling,
Clapped-out saloons and hatchbacks crowd the kerb,
The ubiquitous transistor squawks and gibbers,
The Austins are rust, the golfers mostly dead.
The alders hide an unofficial dump,
Uncaring, the sun still bronzes overhead.

TOO LATE

Too late by far for the William Morris bit,
For homespun commonwealths, the smiling Buddha,
For vegetarian weekends and barn dancing,
For corner co-ops smelling of soap and cheese.
Too late for Moody and Sankey now the devil
No longer bothers to snatch the best of tunes,
Too late, I'm glad to say, for hideous chapels,
Too late for Hollywood and strict tempo trots.

If we're to write it's for the holy fools
Who see beyond the arrogant towers the stars,
Who know our wound is grievous but still sing
That world shall outlast us all and all our error,
That birds build, lovers meet though love be frail,
And actually notice when it's spring.

AFTERNOON AT THE GAUDY

Their gaudy summers leap to life again
As sudden July heat tropics the lawn;
Like giant blooms their skirts enflower the grass,
Chairs nucleate the reminiscing clusters
Of those whose girlhood's now a far fantasia
Of mad May balls, or punting, as apple green
Slow twilight fell over the Oxford spires
And men from Magdalen, Christ's, propelled a dream.

Schoolmistresses, confidential clerks, live organisers
Of village fetes in festive rectory gardens,
Missionaries, artists, sellers of prints and porcelain,
Duty-worn daughters and (let the facts be whispered)
Mistresses, lovers, queue for strawberries
As July sun and sentiment lap them all.

CAMBRIDGE

Tennyson was here, and Byron with his bear,
Here Newton walked, Milton and Rupert Brooke.
It would be easy to grow maudlin over
The banks of Cam in luscious guidebook style.
Reality intrudes, the rare Cambridge sun
Glints on the cameras of the visiting hordes.
Accents of Texas, Tokyo, Timbuctoo,
Insolent French children jostle, shout and run...

Why come at all? The restaurants are full,
The traffic roars, there's nowhere much to park,
The station's miles off, a fen wind appals,
Ubiquitous radios thump the dieseled air.
Because a king, far wiser than he knew,
Raised a stone music that outsoars it all.

13

ANOTHER ENGLAND

Dear Trollope! and dear Barchester! how nice
To read again those cloister intrigues, loathe
The dreadful Slope, the fearful Bishopess,
To read of worldly, wily men of God,
The cello-playing Warden, all the passions
Of High and Low Church wranglings. A small stage
But room enough to weave a pleasing fable
Told to the sound of bells in knick-knacked rooms.

This was another England where the trains
Ran disapproved on Sundays, the world's age
Was just four thousand years, where carriages waited,
Where servants gossiped, gentlemen withdrew
To port and brandy while the ladies plotted,
And God, though served, was seldom contemplated.

ON LONDON BRIDGE AT DUSK

What would you make of this, Will Shakespeare, now
The glistening Thames is topped with brazen towers?
This age of the laser, the electron beam
Scanning our small world's span on a coloured screen?
Your wooden O become a box of tricks
Beyond all Marlowe's fancy or your own?
What would you say now of our cancelled night,
And this tamed river and this poiseless city?

We can but guess, but that superb inseeing
That made your deathless dreams to strut the stage,
That understood the root and fruit of power
Would not be long deceived. Time and the hour
Strike still upon the chimes, hearts break, lusts rage,
Fidelity and forgiveness yet endure.

GRACE

The masters looked up and saw the Heavenly City,
They looked down and they saw it still;
Everywhere, inwardly, outwardly,
The walls and towers were white with grace.

MASTERWORKS

Why does it matter now, at this late date,
Whether Mozart was a mason, or more simply
A fairly lapsed Catholic, or whether he
And Salieri were mortal enemies?
We have what matters most - the great quintets,
A dozen symphonies and a score of other
Masterworks which were wiser than he knew,
Which spring significance from the hasty page.

But what the meaning is... the same is true
Of the unlatined gardener's love of lilies,
The joiner's hand that lifts mere handiness
Into an art, the chap who plants a tree.
Guessed or unguessed the motive is the same.
Known or unknown it's creativity.

BEETHOVEN CHAINED

To be like this! to be in a tower of silence
Held prisoner! Never to hear the lark
Ascend from secret grasses, the roughness of wind
Tearing at rooftops, the trickle of spring streams,
The chatter of market women, the crush of wheels,
The swirl of a silken gown, and worst of all,
To hear no more the piquancy, poignancy of chords,
The dance of canon and fugue, the riot of rondos.

And he master musician, colossal framer
Of sound's architectonics, the bringer-
to-birth of never before heard orders!
Only a god, or a god-intoxicated spirit
Could have borne it, could have called down
Not curses but benedictions calm and still.

16

OPUS 111

The striving of this music! The yearning, the reaching for
That which music longs to incarnate wholly!
Those vistas! Those cloud-citadels!
Those angelic chimeras such as Blake saw
Over ordinary London! Those outbursts
Of blossom as seen on a speeded film!
Those ever-widening ripples on a lake's face
Swan-made and proceeding to infinity!

But this is all metaphor! This says
Only that here we have the unsayable
Striving for speech, for a species of utterance.
The master knew this well and his scrawled symbols
Assembling here to music were for him also
But saying "It is like this. But more, but more..."

ROCOCO

It was an elegant music they made by lakes and gardens
In those palaces under the cloudless summer.
Outside the gilded gates the lodge keepers
Flourished staves at the beggars, drove off the cursing poor.

LONG LIVE THE METAPHYSICAL!

"Eschew the metaphysical," he said.
Easier said than done – there's not much mileage
In pure fact, a catalogue of our assets or
Of what is making us bankrupt, a description
Of gears and cogs and differentials.
"Stick to the prose." But what indeed is that?
Pick up a stone and hold a mystery,
Look in a mirror and behold another!

Apart from which who'd really care to inhabit
The unmetaphysical? Live in a neutered, sad
Entirely tabulated cosmos held
Complete on computer tape or video?
"Long live the metaphysical!" I say.
Without some magic we would all go mad.

A SMALL WORLD

In those days the angels were no metaphors
Or abstract principles or hidden powers.
They might at any hour come to affright
Or pass some message down the straw-strewn nave,
As, from another realm, devils might leap
From cobwebbed corners or from churchyard shadows
Leering, contemning – worse, might come in sleep
To draw the soul out through an eye, an ear.

The world was smaller then and God himself
Not many miles off past the Jovian moons
Could peer in every corner of the parish
Telling some aide to write the sinner down.
The rainbow told his promise overhead
And, undocetic, Christ was real and bled.

AN INTELLIGENT UNIVERSE?

Lusting already for the rape of worlds
Already mapped, and some still posited
Circling some friendly star, imagination
Has hoped for mountains seamed with uranium,
For deserts rich in sulphur, seas full of iodised
And fantastic weeds, has supposed satellites
Platinum-ored, or swarms of minor worlds
Inviting capture, gravid with dividends.

Yet I suspect, and more I hope and pray,
An intelligent universe will not permit
Imperialisms, that natural law forfends
Such impudent hubris, such Icarian folly,
Has, from the first, inbuilt immunity
Against corruption, sets limits, decrees ends.

A REFUSAL

A poet wrote of the morning stars
That they sang together consumed with joy.
I do not want to know the atomic permutations
The astronomer describes for me, the dry mathematics.

ANOTHER CITY

Five minutes to one. Another City morning.
I closed the order book, arranged my tray,
Prepared to see the sun lap Leadenhall.
Yet one more day half-spent, I wondered whether
This was my lot – to catch the 25,
To answer phones and letters, to appear
To care whether commerce prospered and the firm
Again returned a decent dividend.

Another City waited, one of square
And tiny churchyards bright in birdsong still,
Where London Bridge stood barrier to freighters,
Where sunlight whited Dunstan-in-the-East,
And most, where music filled Wren's careful spaces
And Saint Cecilia was Heaven's favourite daughter.

LAST SUPPER

That evening when the moral world was poised
To reverse its polarity He who was and is
The world's desire, and the world's scandal too,
Brought among them the wine rich as rubies
And a strange saying moved upon His lips –
"This is my blood". How could they comprehend
This gnomic thing, this paradox, this riddle?
All this was yet to come, its time not ripe.

Uncomprehending they stored up this word,
One of so many barely understood,
And did not know how soon they would be scattered
Like autumn's loss before the morrow's fury.
Later the image stayed, His strange equation
Moved in their minds. They lived this metaphor.

THE MAN-GOD

Of course we've always known that he was right,
The thousand-day paradox-revelation
The final act; the horror and the hope
Reach to us yet, so that we have to say
This was the Son of God. But humankind
Loves ritual and rite, abjures its freedom;
Give us a book, we cry – a rote, a rule,
Enwrap us with a code which keeps us warm.

And what is this? The publican, the sinner
Dear as the saint, the scholar with his scrolls?
And God Incarnate? How shall matter be
One with the spirit in dynamic tension?
But worst the agony of choice, the stark
Knowledge that acts have infinite dimensions!

THE SHINING

Let me tell of shining things, things that give back
Radiance borrowed from the sun, of steel rails
Narrowing to distance, of glass towers
Rising bronzed and impassive over cities,
Of the gleam of fine porcelain, of the lustre
Of a copper jug, the sheen of wet slates
After the thunder, the air still electric,
Of raindrops prismatic on rose petals.

All these and so many more. The world
Is vibrant with light. Small wonder in faithful days
God was epiphanised in the great rose window.
In prayer and praise his paradigm was this shining –
Intangible, everyday and miraculous –
So many things gracing and all things defining.

WATER LILIES

An archipelago of leaves on flat water,
Subtly coloured, heart-shaped;
And floating, lovely amid these,
The roserich, goldcentred perfection of the waxen water lilies.

CLOTHE ME IN WORDS

And where such beauty was what brilliance now?
And where such innocence what's left unstained?
Eden was once in the harebelled meadows,
Noah's rainbow sang in the swift waterfall.
Still in the eye of lover or poet, still
In the holy folly of the contemplative
The world is a web of glory and wonder
Whose shimmer and colour cry to us for acceptance.

Yes, eye, mind, heart are harrowed and held
Focussed upon horror and heartbreak, hope
Stands mocked by the barbarous and the lover, absurd,
Is butterflied on a wheel of man's fell choices.
Yet, under all, the flower, the star, the bird's
Bright feather and carol cry to me still
      "Clothe me in words!"

PERHAPS IN GARDENS

Perhaps in gardens or at a lake's edge
There's as much wisdom as in seminars,
In the swan's schema or a butterfly's,
In a tree's inscape or the water's rainbows
As in theologies. World is not word.
It is good to rest in the contemplation of roses,
The liquidness of streams, the piscean nature
Of the dumb fish - words will return, and soon.

Word is not world yet sans words how shall we say
What the world tells us even in soliloquy?
To name is in a sense to know, to make discrete
The dazzling imagery too mazey to grasp.
Only one error awaits us, that in the naming
We think that the pointing finger is the moon.

24

ABOUT IN THE QUAD

The minute I mention Him I put myself out of favour.
Clever young folk who've done their PPE
Know that serious thinkers dismiss Him out of hand
(A meaningless answer to a meaningless question).
Editors reach for the out tray – we can't sell that
To a generation weaned on Wittgenstein.
Nonconformist, I expect the new orthodoxy
To contemn my heresy and to smile their dismissals.

As for me I say to hell with your orthodoxy!
I will not equate *pensee* with pansy,
I will not concern myself with SW3 or 7.
I have heard Bach tell me that the heart of this odd
World beats soundly under our fury and folly
And God or Someone is certainly about in the quad.

A DIVINE PATIENCE

It says, I feel, something for God that he
Out-tops this flummery, these dreadful hymns,
The treacly *vox humana*, the tired chords,
The dressing up, the platitudinous pep talk.
Somehow it seems he manages to find
A corner still in the sad hearts of folk
Who sense there's something more, insinuates
His way into their real and daily needs.

Strange to consider that this weekly outing
For clerical egos and these ritual cleansings
Are said to be for Him who took on flesh
And walked with those rejected, lectured, blamed,
Spurning those dealers in the ceremonial
Who thought their rote and rite had got him tamed.

UNDERSTANDING

"Sir," said the disciple, "speak me the one word which is wisdom;
Tell me the one word which is all knowledge".
No word passed the Master's lips:
After much frowning, suddenly the disciple smiled.

A PRIMAL CRY OF JOY

Damn the science of it - the temperature, duration of daylight,
The clock in the genes! I hear the blackbird utter
His first call of the year, that well-remembered,
That unlike-all-other sound. Say if you like
It can all be plotted and graphed, it is nothing but
This or that. It is all the same a wonder
Of blended notes and, though brief, is prophetic
Of so much more to come, come the equinox.

No. I'll believe it is a primal cry of joy,
Of welcome even, of anticipation,
Of becoming after a dim, slow-blooded season
Sensible of the quickening ray of the sun
As the being of earth stirs, responds
To the lord star of our corner of creation.

I CAN NO OTHER

The genes, the unconscious, are not half of it.
Freud, Marx and all the rest cannot begin
To tell why for their music's sake, their art's,
So many say "This I must surely do,
I can no other". And no threats, no pains
Deter them, make them doubt, still less retract
What's known to them as surely as the sun.
They have their imperatives which they must obey.

Let fools suppose the state has prior claims
Or some daft cause demands their blood and breath,
Let lunatics preach dementia, to the flames
Consign the poem, play the fool with reason,
A few, a blessed few, will always say
"My truth I speak, my prophecy I proclaim".

NORMAN NICHOLSON: *In Memoriam*

In Wordsworth's country you avoided Wordsworth's
Tendentiousness and did not moralise
Over the hill folk and the astonishing mountains,
Told us rather of the walled and Celtic fields
In that land of small chapels and landmarks,
Of strewn stone and sudden, luscious valleys
Dairied and emerald by the heads of lakes,
Of the long–lying snow and the saving cairns.

You peopled your land with creatures
As real and plain as the boulders,
Loved too the small, gritty towns and the sea–edged mills,
Saw here a place where among humble people
Innocent of theophanies Christ and his band of brothers
Walked still, preaching against the age and the grain of man.

UNREGARDED MIRACLES

The readiness, the openness is all;
The poetry is there for the looking.
Sun, grass, rainfall, stars, moonlight,
The unregarded miracles, always await celebration.

CHRIST OF CHARING CROSS

Warm from the afterglow of Elgar's vast
And towering symphony we leave the hall
And cross the bridge beside the thundering trains.
The mist is wraith-like on the silent Thames,
The night is beautiful, we hold hands in love
Of music, of the town and of each other.
But under archways there are huddled sacks
With eyes and hands, and cartons serve for beds.

The derelicts of London whose cold comfort
On clammy nights is under these grim girders!
With soup and bread the helpers proffer warmth
Worth more than a hundred sermons. Christ moves here unseen,
God's thief in the London dark, at Charing Cross
Where Francis Thompson saw him walk the water.

ANOTHER COMING

When they have had their way, those who suppose
God an eternal social worker, an undying
Utopian, the great cathedrals will stand empty
Of all that is numinous, remaining only
As museums of primitive art or auditoria
For symphony orchestras or boys with guitars.
The holy flame will be snuffed in the sanctuary,
The altar moved to facilitate access.

And God will come into his own again.
He will smile on the face of the waters and his chime
Will be the rising of Sirius, his balm the moonlight;
He will move in the hearts of the lover and the child,
He will rejoice in his new poverty, His voice
Will be the croo-crooing of doves, the triumphant sun his flight.

PARADOX

Love came down from celestial spheres
To be crucified like a murderer.
Love is tender, vulnerable, terribly frail;
Is strong as the seas, mighty as mountains and as eternal.

UNDER GOD'S SHADOW

Why should I strive with words and images?
When it comes down to it these poems are written
Under God's shadow. Could it be otherwise?
Who or what else is worthy of our desire?
The best of us deserve commending only
For our best impulses. Whose charity but God's
Could endure us, we the flawed, the wilful-blind,
His wonder-children tinkering with his fire?

Say what you will there's little health in us
Nor hope nor love nor beauty but contends
With counter-currents of self-will, self-praising
And in the end self-hatred, self-despair.
By what are we redeemed but by the godlike
Striving to out, crying *Kyrie Eleison!*

DISCLAIMER

So what is all this about the heroic priesthood
Of the writer? the artist? For me, let truth be told,
To assume that mantle would be simple fraud.
I write because I always have, and say
What I feel worth the saying or worth praising,
Less often what deserves contempt or laughter.
But hero? No. Priest? Hardly. Why
Claim loftier functions than I'm fitted for?

Only from conceit or from the false perspectives
Of self-induced manias, bogus paradises
Or alcoholic nightmare some make claim
To holy orders. Better to rise and shine
As best one may, be lover, husband, friend,
Listen to Bach, read Trollope, walk by the sea
And mildly regret one's ordinary vices.

II Nevertheless Through Grasses

MERVYN LINFORD

For Clare and Robert

Mervyn Linford has contributed to a number of magazines
including *Acumen, Envoi, Essex Countryside, Orbis,
Outposts, PN Review, The Countryman* and *The London
Magazine.* His poetry has also been broadcast on national
and local radio. He has received several awards, including:
1st prize, Hastings National Open Competition 1984.
3rd prize, Douglas Gibson Memorial Competition 1986.
1st prize, John Clare Open Competition 1989.
He has lived in Essex since early childhood and is a
member of Southend Poetry Group.

Nevertheless through Grasses is a collection of 37 poems,
some of which have previously appeared in magazines.
It expresses with acute observation and powerful
imagery the author's perceptions of his native county –
its landscapes, natural history and people.

CONTENTS

WATERCOLOUR

By an island in the Crouch –
Where the widgeon whistle
And the slow, slouch tide
Catches the fire
Of the falling sunlight –
Where the windows
In a wooden shack
Blaze to the blueness
Of a frosted sky
And their tide-wrack embers
Delve into doubles
On the dowse of river.

By an island in the Crouch –
Where the buoys bob yellow
Through the brine of dusk
And the sea-silk oils
Slide through the shallows
Into silts and saltings –
Where the wide, wet marshes
Cast their reflections
In a web of water
And the far, flute curlew
Curve, like a calmness
To the moon's momentum.

STRANDED

A trawler runs aground –
Straddles the slipway,
Like a spent whale.

Waves keep pounding in –
Nuzzle and gnaw
At the shattered timbers.

People in small shoals
Swim through the eddies
Of their disbelief.

Cameras click,
And words, like flotsam,
Drift on the currents
Of a loud amazement.

A furl of sand
Is hoisted by the gale –
Flutters to landward
On a squall of voices.

LAPWINGS

Sometimes, when spring, like a green idea,
Dispenses with winter and its icy reason –
When the season's instinct
Proffers a flower to enamoured bees
And leaves between showers
Whisper their secrets to flirtatious light;

Then may you see them, on the skittish air,
Those careless plovers
Cresting their passion on erratic wings –
High, in their raptures of rhapsodic flight
As they climb, but to tumble
From the sun's seduction;

Then may you see them, in the wind's embrace
As they cry, like derision,
Over jilted pasture –
Where the sky, made frantic
By their fleet attention,
Clings, like a lover, to each thin proposal.

BEANFLOWERS

Autumn impinges, even though it's spring:
        just a word - "beanflowers";
"Late last year," she said,
"Too late to come to anything".

How does a word hold so much power?
No need to close my eyes, to concentrate;
The scarlet blooms just grow there, like a vision.

I can feel the heat, the calm October weather:
Chrysanthemums and dahlias, bleaching in sunlight -
        smoke, like a blue ghost,
Climbing the trellis into air unfathomed.

        What now?
The daffodils have tarnished in the shadows -
        turned to rust.
Tulips, like closed fists,
Suffer with their swollen veins -
        ease into redness.

She leaves her seat to walk across the lawn -
        tugs at a few weeds.
The early bees are cumbersome with sound -
A swallow cuts a corner, clings, like ice.

BIRD NESTING

I recall a blackbird's nest, hidden in brambles:
A woven cup of mud and grass –
Protected by the whiplash briars.

How great the temptation –
Four smooth eggs, blue-green and mottled brown.

I didn't mind the scratches –
The beads of blood,
Smeared to a trickle down the arms and legs;

It was a clutch of treasure –
A test, something to be proud of.

I used a thorn to pierce the shell, then blew –
Nothing came, no thick translucence, no pallid yolk.

The air around rattled with the parent's chiding;
The shell peeled whitely to the foetal flesh –
To the small, pink bud, barely pulsating.

EEL

Essence of evil from the far Sargasso –
Spilling its unction into dykes and ditches.

Sheened into slithers, under shales of light –
Oozes its cryptic into pond and river.

Elver to adult through a twist of years –
Adding its inches by the wrench of flesh.

Tunnel of dark blood, coil of questions,
Helix of a deep existence.

Wriggle of something in the silts of sleep –
Brim to the margins of our dry defences.

Spinner of concepts, like an involution –
Draws the pretences to the spawn of being.

MAY THE FIFTH

The arrival of the swifts –
For days I've watched,
        nothing;
And yet there they are,
Five on the evening air –
Curved into substance
By the thought of summer.

Cuniform on blue papyrus –
Fluent with contrast;
All night they'll fly –
Ink to the sky's ink,
Lost to the liquid
Of the leaching stars.

        Tomorrow,
When the flowers wake –
When the words of fragrance
Climb on the voices
Of the warming earth;
They'll underline
The languages they make –
Screech over paper,
Like a nib that scratches.

SWALLOW

The swallow complies with physics –
is both wave and particle.

It follows on from air –
visits awareness, like an apparition.

Fire and blue–steel both –
tempered by sunlight
and the slake of water.

Spirit and substance:
it flies to its dual ends –
mind over matter to the tips of feathers.

A ghost in oscillations over wheat,
that resonates with everything that's summer.

WHEN

When I walk through the graveyard to the river's bank --
Between the tilted headstones, heavy with lichen,
And the rusted iron crosses,
    leaning at irreverent angles;

    I am thankful only, for the lack of care:
For the red-dead-nettles,
Sprawling in their purple vestments –
For the blue-eyed speedwell,
Turning its iris to the lifting sun;
    And for the trees above me,
        spreading their fleeces to the dove's syllabic.

LIONS AND LAMBS

The high elms, snap wood
against the March wind.

Elated rooks, race and revel
in their spring debate.

A prowl of cloud, rages
in ferocious sky;

and the timid fields
chase through the shadows
on a bleat of flowers.

STARS OF BETHLEHEM
(Ulting Church, Essex: grave of a child burnt to death
 accidentally in the nineteenth century)

Shattered, is the peace of Sunday –
The river's glass turns fragments in the wake
Of every craft that cuts its thin resistance.

Somewhere a child laughs
And the sound's sharp pitch
Scratches the surface of a lucid moment.

I turn towards the church –
Walk quietly, like a ghost, across the grass,
To where a few small stars
Brink from the borders of neglected graves.

Somewhere a child laughs –
No-one hears, so no-one answers.

Doves in a low dirge
Cloud the perceptions through a trance of leaves;
And the slow light dancing
Delves to the shadows of inscripted stone.

LANDING

Walk out again:
look at the marshes –
the sweep of the sea-wall.

Imagine what it was like
to live there, or there;
different time, different weather.

The rooks create a marquetry:
black against blue ground –
movement in the year's first stillness.

You can smell the heat –
feel it, like a memory.

A barge lies broken on the mud –
ribs and vertebra; shattered, prehistoric.

Crabs move sideways –
scuttle in irons.

A shelduck curves to laughter up the reach –
spreads out its wings; cuts swarf from water.

NEVERTHELESS THROUGH GRASSES

Saying that the sun speaks
that its words are waves
decipherable
in peaks
and troughs
and distances
is helpful if the eyes
are cut like prisms
if our religion
is divisible from whiteness
and the rainbow bends
through definite degrees

when the lark is infinity
or almost
a pencil-point
a full-stop
for its own song
then our differences
are air and gravity
are longings
for the impossible

nevertheless through grasses
where the adder curves
where the burnet-moth
and the skipper
stir through the shimmers
of incessant heat
and the ranunculus
like butter
bleats its pathetic pollen

then is it reasonable to ask
then when the tongue
like the swallow's tail
forks over summer
with its sweet surmisals
when the bee beats
on incredulous wings
and the moon like honey
climbs the horizon
of our dark misgivings.

BREAM

Browser in bubbles:
Dumb to the power of its own momentum –
Flanking the silence with a slab that silvers.

Hump-headed into many facets –
Delver in darkness, like a thousand mirrors.

Clouder of clear streams, stirrer of weeds:
A down-deep sow of a fish –
Herding and haunting through a swirl of fins.

Breaker of a tense meniscus –
Thudding from fathoms to the thump of water.

Plunger and poker through a gorge of silt –
Grinding the gravid with a throat of teeth.

CUTTING

How we loved that embankment -
To clamber through the hot, oppressive air,
Logging the numbers of the self-same engines.

To lie contented in the grass -
Those bread and sugar hours,
With the great moon-daisies

Nodding above us, with an eye for insects.
There, we would place our pennies on the track -
Heady with mischief

And the whiff of danger.
The smell of coal and tar,
Thick and pervasive in a glaze of light -

The whirr of wires through rings and pulleys,
As the shifting signals
Clattered their message on the tilt of iron.

So far away, those ant-infested slopes:
Lizards and slow-worms -
Evasive, with the loss of tails;

The passengers, with time enough to wave,
And the steam's dank texture -
Cool and condensing, like the bloom on damsons.

WILLOW CUTTING

More like autumn than summer:
the men, cutting willows –
burning branches.

Smoke lies thick across the river:
the wheat-fields, gold –
the distance, blueish.

I watch the moorhens in the shallows:
ticking, like clockwork –
heads nodding.

The terns are on patrol:
hovering an instant –
dipping to their own reflections.

Swallows will soon be gathering:
swifts already gone –
the cuckoo also.

Spiderlings are lofted under silk:
rise on the warming air –
drift in dispersals.

Soon the geese in gaggles will return:
skeins on a blue glaze –
cracks in the pattern.

NEW TOWN

How the town was then
in its slow sleep
never again
to be found ungrowing
in the sky-wet
weep of the leaves
over slippery paths
where the sly smell
reeks and remembers
of a fox-brown autumn
there, where the rank air
turns on its tendrils
to a twine of ivy
and the blue-black
sloes in the hedgerows
bend over brambles
on a bloom of berries
never again
in the sun-slick
sheen over water
and the wisp of willows
where the branch-bare
rooks in a revel
pepper with purple
the surrounding elms
what of the witch
and the one-eyed man
in the ditch-dark
path by the windows
of their lamp-lit hovels
where the moon's arc
climbs from the copses
on the lips of owls
and the bat's wing
sweeps like a besom
through a blink of shadows

there, in the star-still
step of Orion
over half the sky
as the light's chill
cools and condenses
to the wink of frost
there, in the lost land
in the long past
moss and the mildew
of another ruin
in the snow-soft
rut-hard
white of a winter
that has gone forever
what of the spring
and the waiting sisters
of the goose-grey
cold into April
and the clutch of Easter
of their old age
shell-thin
frail in the fortune
of an ancient holding
what of the sun
and the scent of summer
of the dog-rose
dog-star
death and denial
of their golden harvest.

Awarded first prize, John Clare Poetry Competition 1989

BLUE TIT

Euclidean bird; scholar of the easy angle –
Logician of the cylinder and sphere.

Fat-shredder, foil-shearer:
Hangs upside down and dangles like a fact
To any quirk or querisome devisal.

Fledge-fellow, flit-fraction:
Yellowness that measures like a mote,
Then disappears in blue's matriculation.

Nut-nudger, rind-razor:
Gauge and gyration on the plumb of lines –
Swinging its ounceless to a lead that lessens.

Eye-striper, hole-filler:
Solution to the caterpillar's loop –
Geometer that balances equations.

HOMESTEADER

We used to drive his old jalopies –
        over the fields, the unmade roads.

Get in a rut and you'd stay there,
        like a needle in a groove.

Every week, the same music:
Gangsters on the running-boards –
        Fangio, behind the wheel.

They say he was backward:
Preferred the company of children –
        enjoyed their games.

He didn't seem silly to me –
        not when he gave us sweets, money.

His two old aunts kept ducks and chickens:
We used to steal their eggs –
        cook them on the camp-fire.

Once, we took his bicycle –
        sold it to the gypsies.

He never knew it was us:
        still played our games –
                forked-out for friendship.

OIL-MEN

I didn't believe in cowboys, until I saw them -
Fresh out of Texas, to this Essex pipeline.

Ten-gallon hats, check shirts
And leather boots; welders mostly,
Loud and aggressive with their "Howdy pardners!"

Their foreman was the straw-boss;
Loudest of all in his mini-moke,
Yelling his orders, like a big-time rancher.

They didn't need a bunk-house -
The best hotels, the prime cuts.

I think they saw us as apaches;
Primitives with totems and taboos -
Indigenous, but dumb and out of date.

"Hey, you boy, get off yer butt, godammit!"
I did my best to sidestep the lassoes -
Though being quaint, my hide was ripe for iron.

MAN HUNGRY: HUNGRY MAN

"What a broad!"
        he said,

And I thought of Norfolk
And a pot of eels.

"No! a perfect chick!"
        he said,

And quick as a dough
The metaphor was mixed;
Duckling, I thought,
        spit-roasted,
Followed by goose-gog pie.

"No! a real tasty bird!"
        he said,

And Norfolk turkey
Steamed in the stirring
Of the mind's rich pudding.

"No!" he said,
"A round, ripe, ravenous tart!"

Time for dinner thought I –
All this sexist talk
Churns in the stomach
        like a lover's spoon.

MIDDLE AGE

I borrowed me brother's double-breasted,
Just the number for the weekly dance;
Whether it went with the hound's-tooth check,
The winkle-pickers, I wouldn't like to say;
I felt good though, in with a chance,
      Know what I mean?

Sixteen, hair slicked back, Tony Curtis,
Duck's arse, fag at a leery angle;
I wasn't much of a dancer, held back
You know, waited for the slow ones;
I can't remember her name, Maisie or Pat,
      I'm not sure now.

Anyhow, you know the type, hooped skirts,
Masses of petticoats, stockings and suspenders;
Funny, it didn't seem erotic then,
Lust was purer in those days;
Anyway, enough of that old nonsense,
      On with the story.

AMAZONIAN CLONE PARABLE

Adam and Evil were naked,
"an apple a day," said the snake,
with a sort of hippocratic malevolence.

Evil said, "I'd sooner be beauty",
So Adam bit her ear
and she became deaf to the core.

Adam found his looks adorable –
couldn't give a fig for God
and saw himself the object of reflection.

Evil said, that Adam was a madam –
Adam fell madly in love
with the suggestion, and drowned.

Evil, by herself, was sorry for ribbing Adam
and made amends by wearing a robe
and becoming immaculate.

When she gave birth to her own father's son,
she was confused –
could not conceive of parthenogenesis.

The doctor blamed the symptoms on neurosis:
she knew a snake-in-the-grass, when she saw one –
she sloughed her skin; turned ugly, with genetics.

ALL FLESH IS GRASS : MOW DOWN A VEGETARIAN

We have a wholemeal sensibility –
An organic preference.

My wife is willing, you could say –
Happy, with a vegetable existence.

She soaks her pulses well –
Resists the flesh in favour of the bean.

Sometimes, when in need of roughage,
We test our fibre to the nerve's last straw –
Take muesli to its limits.

Once, before decaffeinated coffee –
Between T'ai–chi and meditation;
We made a record of achievements.

She said, it was good to be good –
That peas and lentils were closer to the Gods.

I said, that I agreed; that cows were sacred
And people should be satisfied with legumes.

We knew, that there was room for all –
That greediness was tantamount to meat,
And grass the dilemma of our ruminations.

ST BENET'S SHEEP

If you go to St Benets, or is it Benedicts?
      Where the old red mill
Grows from the arches of the abbey's ruins;

You may, as I, a stranger on this road
Whose dusty way is lined with Norfolk reeds;
Be slow at first, to hear the voice of prayer
That leaves the wind and feathers through the marsh;

But if you stand and stare across the Bure,
Where sails, in supplication, search the sky
And harriers hang cruciform on air;

You may, just once, be conscious in a while
Of how the past in plainsong lingers there
And why the geese, in gaggles, crop the sward.

HEAVENWARDS

There's not much grace
When a swan takes wing –
What with faith
And gravity in opposition
And the skin of water
Losing its tension
To the webbed assault;

It's hard to think
Of anything like finesse,
When every thought
Has laughter as its link
To test the bonds
Of beauty and deportment;

But when it springs
Long-headed into flight,
Beyond the walk
Absurdly over waves,
It brings to earth
An aspect of delight
That names itself
The element of angels.

THAMES BARGE

Out there she lies, sedately on the tide,
A legacy of dim-departed seas;
The block across the horse* begins to slide
As fill the sails aslant the western breeze.

An evening fades to ochre on the ebb
As down the dredge she drifts towards the east –
She rides the waves, a bluff and blunted head,
Across the shoals to far-forgotten quays.

And we are there, our memories abaft,
To haul the sheet and leave the land behind –
To tack upon the swatchways of the past,
Beyond the shallow moorings of the mind.

Yes, we are there, a sheer above the silt,
A ripple on the passage of our days;
Our wake is cut beneath the spirit's keel
And every moon diminished by its phase.

*Horse: an iron bar athwart the stern, allowing the mainsail
block to move freely along its length, from port to starboard.

HUNTER'S MOON

This a night
   for the river.
Not a word's breath
   quivers its question
      through unanswered leaves.
The silence
   listens to itself –
Sinks to the echo
   of inverted vision.
A mist
   transliterates
      from   air –
Layers its language
   with a level tongue.
Somehow
     the stars
        resist –
Shift their assumptions
   into iridescence.
The moon reflects
   a virtue of its own –
     mouths the phonetic
         into double zero.

STARLING

Master of mimics out of clicks and murmurs:
Street-curlew, phone-caller –
Ghost at the corner of contrary skies,
Hawking the habit of its clone accoustics.

Slang-shuffler, kerb-coster:
Rooster on ledges in the sleaze of neon –
Hunching its shoulders to the inch of hustle.

Bunce-blagger, nest-knocker:
Spiv in the market of plebian sparrows –
Touting the traffic of its sway and swagger.

Crowd-pusher, beak-stabber:
Shifty in winter with a bib of blizzards –
Slick into summer, with its suit a spectrum.

GREYSCAPE: THAMES ESTUARY

Here, no romantic wave-talk,
No shell's voice
For the tide to infiltrate.

The air, after heavy rain,
Smells like ditchwater
And imagination
  lays claim upon immunity.

Nothing's of importance
When grey is realised;
Attitudes of dull sky
Argue with sea
  for their own discernment,
And gulls between nowhere
Worry, like language
            in their isolation.

CAPTAIN

Never saw a ship, but liked the uniform –
Swung on his gate, white hat and gold braid,
For all the world a salt retired.

"Morning mates!
Good weather for a trip,
Wind's in the right quarter."

We never thought it strange,
Eccentric perhaps, but harmless –
His house, a craft of sorts,
Chimneys under full smoke,
An orchard, thick with masts and yards.

I've seen him list through a tide of cabbages –
Rolling to landward under swigs of rum.

"Drop a grog me hearties,
Come aboard,
I'll spin yer a yarn."

We never went, lubbers to a man –
The last I remember was a wreck of limbs,
Sprawled by the windfalls, in a sea of bottles.

CLIFFTOWN

A Wednesday afternoon, the summer in retreat
And autumn's tune, not rousing like a march,
But beat by beat through colours of detachment.

The quiet streets are cast in such a light
That scours stone and bleaches stubborn brick;
Until, though each so different to the eye,
Become as one in subtleties of yellow.

The bowling-green, is peopled and apart –
Composed as if a score upon a sheet,
Where shadows mark the tempo of the leaves
That drop their notes, like brass, diminuendo.

DILUVIAL

The river's in flood again –
has had enough
of summer's slow meander.

It inundates the fields –
pretends a sea
Where cattle sailed all year

and swished their tails
through semaphores of sunlight.
November's clouds

are wrung by sullen hands –
are fists of scud
that beat the season's bounds

and drown the leaves, unhinged
by prone sou'westers.
The gulls drift far inland –

flake down, like snow
incongruous with sound,
to settle on the shrub-infested waters.

A rift of gold
turns wavelets into scales –
a sudden fish, that leaps, and then submerges.

BLOW-OUT

A funny bloke is autumn -
A rare old windbag,
All smoke and bluster.

A brown-ale swill of a man,
Frowning to furrows
In the dregs of sunlight.

He's had his fill of goodness -
Can barely stand,
So heavy with excesses.

Listen, to the way he moans -
How the next drawn breath
Whistles and wheezes
On the weight of weather.

See, how he staggers
With his load -
How his sack-full swagger
Bellies and buckles
With the heft of plenty.

He knows the score -
Has seen before
December's brittle ghost,
Hoary and heartless
With a fist of splinters.

Knows well the boast
Of swallows on the wing -
Wefting, like shuttles,
From the warp of winter.

Awarded first prize, Hastings Open Competition 1985

ELIM LIL

Elim Lil, evangelist in a tin shack –
       Poor Clare to rats and magpies.
Said prayers aloud –
   sang hymns beneath eccliastic branches.
A paradise to her:
   bullace and greengage,
      bread for the small birds,
        plums for an autumn eucharist.
The children used to watch her
             at the well –
Rebecca in a shift of rags.
Perhaps there was some latter-day
            St Francis –
Some loss of love remembered and revered
That turned her heart
      from earth's dissatisfactions.
Selfless, yet sufficient:
Vegetables and cottage flowers,
Timber, cut and stacked against the frost.
On winter nights the sacrament of candles –
The votive glare from windows otherworldly.

ELIM: Evangelical Light Mission

Awarded third prize, Douglas Gibson Memorial Competition 1986

DECEMBER RAIN

The weather changes for the worse –
   turns wet and mild.

All thoughts of snow have thawed –
The mind, like ice, dissolving under rain.

The seasonal denial, tradition thwarted –
Not even frost or starlight to expose
That winter need for unaccustomed whiteness.

   The arthritic trees complain –
Gesticulate in grey, prevailing torment.

The sullen clouds, like cynical balloons,
Deflate at dusk and saturate the senses.

FROST APPLES

The apple-tree has lost its leaves:
The yellow fruits are luminous –
Are lanterns to the old wassailing ghosts
Whose forms we see evolving from our breath.

The fieldfares and the redwings, less deceived,
Just scavenge through the windfalls in the frost;
A phantom moon hangs gibbous in the east –
Epiphany in blue before the stars.